# The Financial Buffet

## A Smorgasbord of Retirement Planning Lessons from the World Around Us

### JOHN STILLMAN

ISBN: 1548246506
ISBN-13: 978-1548246501

# DEDICATION

To Molly, who still takes me to a buffet for my birthday every year, even though she'd rather dine on shoe leather.

To Lilly and Amos, without whom this book would have been completed at least two years earlier.

# CONTENTS

# INTRODUCTION

I love a good buffet.

I remember one particular trip to a buffet (Western Steer, I believe it was) when I was a kid. I couldn't have been more than eight years old. I was so blown away by the mind-bending array of options in front of me that I felt compelled to eat a heaping helping of basically everything they had to offer. After several plates, I was miserable, but determined to get through my bowl of ice cream.

I was only a few bites away from finishing when I looked at my parents and said, "I feel like I'm going to throw up."

And I did, right there in my ice cream.

I do remember feeling a lot better after that and I wanted to go get another bowl of ice cream to replace the one that I'd just ruined, but my parents informed me that I was finished eating for the day. In fact, I remember Dad's statement: "You know, even pigs stop eating before they throw up."

A valuable lesson was learned that day, and it remains the only time that I've ever actually eaten myself to the point of retching.

While that's clearly the most memorable buffet-related anecdote in my arsenal, it really has nothing to do with this book. In fact, this book has nothing to do with food at all. You see, the reason that I really love a buffet has nothing to do with the opportunity to consume enormous amounts of food. It's really about the *variety*. If you're ordering dinner from a menu, it's highly unlikely that you'll have the opportunity to enjoy a big salad, a bite of

i

seven different kinds of meat, six different side dishes, some fresh fruit, and a yeast roll. You could do it, but your dinner would probably cost $60.

But at a buffet, you can sample a little bit of everything for a reasonable price. The variety is unparalleled in any other dining experience.

This book is also about variety. There's a seemingly endless number of financial and retirement planning lessons that can be learned from the world around us, and we'll explore a fraction of them in these pages.

In one section of the financial buffet, we have financial lessons learned from life in general. In another section, lessons from some famous quotable people. In yet another section, we'll explore financial principles to be gleaned from old television shows. And we'll conclude with lessons that I've learned from people that I've met—some who became clients, and some who didn't.

As you read, my goals for you are two-fold. First, I hope you enjoy the variety of stories and learn a valuable principle or two along the way. Second, I hope this book doesn't make you throw up in your ice cream.

# SECTION I:

# Financial Lessons from Everyday Life

# 1 THE WRONG SUIT

My friend Zack got married on a crisp March day in Greenville, South Carolina. He's the life of the party wherever he goes, so he has a deep pool of friends. I was one of his 11 groomsmen.

We'd all ordered matching suits from Jos A Bank (believe it or not they had a special going on). We were told that the suits would be shipped to our house and then we'd just need to go get them tailored.

As of two weeks before the wedding, I still hadn't gotten a suit. So, I stopped by Jos A Bank to see what was up. After they called around to a couple of different stores and eventually got in touch with FedEx to track the shipping, we determined that the suit had actually been shipped to my old house in Hillsborough. I hadn't lived there in three years, but Zack apparently didn't have my current address so that's what he gave them. So, I had to make the 25-minute drive up to my old house and knock on their door. Sure enough, my suit had been sitting in a box in their living room for three weeks while they tried to figure out what they were supposed to do with it.

So now I was in a rush to get it tailored so that I could get it back in time. Picked it up just a day before the wedding and stuck it in my closet with a full 24 hours to spare. Crisis averted.

Fast forward to the wedding day. The wedding party was supposed to be at the venue two hours before the ceremony. So, there's all 11 of the groomsmen hanging out in the parking lot. We'd been there about an hour when Sam grabbed my jacket sleeve and held it up next to his.

"Why do our suits look different?" he wanted to know.

They looked similar, but they were slightly different colors, and definitely a different texture. I looked around. His suit looked like everybody else's, mine didn't. So, I peeked inside at my tag.

Van Heusen. Not Jos A Bank.

After all the rushing around and driving to Hillsborough and paying extra to expedite the tailoring, I'd grabbed the wrong suit out of my closet when I was packing to leave the house. And now I was almost four hours from home with a wedding starting in an hour, and I'm in the wrong suit.

Suffice it to say that the rest of the guys got a hearty laugh out of it. We decided that we wouldn't be mentioning this to the bride just yet. It's something that we decided would be funny to her in a few weeks, but not at that moment.

It turned out to not be a big deal. It was one of those situations where you wouldn't really know that something was amiss unless you were specifically looking for it. I was the tallest of the 11 groomsmen, so I was at the far end of the line during the ceremony, seemingly a football field away from Zack.

And let's be honest. Nobody at a wedding is paying any attention to Groomsman #11.

So other than the people in attendance that I couldn't resist telling about the mishap, nobody knew the difference.

But in a lot of ways, that whole situation reminds me of a retirement plan.

In any given year (assuming your portfolio is invested intelligently), you're going to have some investments that perform incredibly well. And you're going to have some that aren't looking so great—investments that are wearing the wrong suit, if you will.

But that's ok. Because the next year, the investment that performed incredibly well this year might be in the toilet. And this year's stinker might be the winner next year. That's why you don't go all-in on any one particular strategy.

To quote my friend Bob Payne, the managing director of Payne Capital Management, "I don't know what asset class is going to be up in value next year, but I know that our portfolios are going to own some of it."

If you're having a wedding, it's inevitable that *something* is going to go wrong along the way. (Hopefully I won't be the one responsible for it every time). But if the sound system is working and the bride doesn't trip and fall and the food is good, nobody is going to give a second thought to the goober in the wrong suit at the end of the line of groomsmen.

In your portfolio, it's inevitable that you're going to have something that goes wrong. But as long as you planned well, you're going to have a lot more things that turn out just fine.

Anyway, sorry about that, Zack and Nicole. I'm sure you'll still make beautiful children anyway.

## 2 AN OSCAR-WINNING RETIREMENT

My wife Molly asked if it would bother me if she had the Oscars on the TV in our room while I drifted off to sleep. I couldn't think of a more sleep-inducing television experience than a bunch of self-congratulatory Hollywood communists patting each other on the back and giving shout-outs to their middle school drama teacher who believed in them when no one else did. So I was happy to oblige that request.

I did slightly wake up about an hour later when she started yelling "WHAT IS HAPPENING RIGHT NOW??" But I was still more interested in sleeping, so I just rolled back over and didn't think anything of it.

When I woke up the next morning, Twitter was ablaze with a bunch of jokes that I didn't understand. After I finally saw the footage, the jokes started to make sense.

As it turned out, the producers of a movie called *La La Land* spent about two minutes basking in the glory of their "Best Picture" victory before the red carpet got pulled out from under them and they had to cede the stage to the rightful winners, the producers of a movie called *Moonlight*. They handled it with as much dignity and class as anyone could have asked for, but you *know* that it felt like a punch in the gut.

Unfortunately, I've seen retirement pan out roughly the same way for people who didn't do adequate planning.

It usually looks something like this…

You announce to everyone at work that you're retiring. Some are jealous of you, others are genuinely happy for you, and some seem to be outwardly happy but are actually jealous and don't want you to know it. But there's a lot of uproar and cake and congratulatory Hallmark cards and then you ride off into the sunset. The trophy is yours.

Maybe a year goes by. Or it could be several years. But then you start hearing this little whisper in the back of your head that says, "Hey bud, unless you die a lot sooner than you're planning to, you're going to run out of money."

"But I had almost a million dollars," you say. "Isn't that plenty?"

You go on for another few months and the whisper turns into a much louder voice.

So you go to visit a financial advisor. You talk about how much you don't miss your job and the trip you took to Europe and the 14-pound catfish that you caught in the mountains last weekend. And then the conversation turns to your portfolio and you discover that the whisper-turned-shout was actually right all along. You're going to run out of money.

You're now faced with a choice. You can either significantly reduce the quality of your lifestyle for your remaining years, or you can go back to work.

And now you find yourself in the same boat as the *La La Land* producers— you're giving back your retirement trophy that you only got to hold for a couple of minutes before somebody came along and told you that you didn't actually win. You try to handle it with dignity and class, but there's no denying that it's a gut punch.

Imagine how things would have been different if Warren Beatty had been handed the correct envelope and he'd simply read *Moonlight* as the winner from the very beginning. Sure, the *La La Land* guys would have been disappointed that they didn't win, but they wouldn't have had to endure the pain of having that momentary taste of euphoria only to have it yanked away moments later.

Now, imagine if you'd started working with a competent planner and constructed a well-conceived retirement plan a few years before you actually retired. You would have discovered that you actually *couldn't* retire at the age you were planning, and while you would have been disappointed, at least you would have found out in advance. So you continue working for an extra couple of years, nobody else knows any different, and then you can eventually retire and enjoy the lifestyle that you wanted…instead of enjoying it temporarily only to have it taken away later.

The bottom line is that I'm constantly amazed by the number of people who waltz off into retirement without a real understanding of whether or not they're retiring at the right time, or any inkling of how much they can legitimately spend each year once they no longer have a paycheck.

So just be sure you're holding the right envelope. It's much better for everyone that way.

# 3 THE BABY IN THE FRONT SEAT

"I really hope that's a doll and not an actual baby," I told my wife, Molly.

We were headed east on I-40 when I saw the baby's head leaned up against the window. The van was in the lane to our left and a couple of car lengths ahead of us. There were a couple of older kids in the back, but we just couldn't quite tell if that was a real baby in the front seat or not.

We assumed that it was probably a doll because of the position of the head. If it was a baby, that would be a really awkward way to be holding it (as if there's a way to hold a baby in the front seat of a minivan traveling 75 mph on the interstate that *isn't* awkward).

So after an initial panic, we came to the conclusion that it was just a doll. No need to alert the authorities.

And then…it moved.

The baby's head moved! It was now clear that this wasn't a doll. This was a baby.

We started discussing our options. Are we supposed to alert the local gendarme? Do we just mind our own business and let these wildly irresponsible folks go about their day? What's the protocol for this?

As we were mulling over our options, the van merged over in front of us. So, I took the opportunity to pull over into the left lane and pull up beside them so that Molly could at least give them a nasty look.

As soon as we got up beside them, Molly looked over, prepared to give her most scornful, judgmental you-can't-possibly-be-serious scowl.

And then she started laughing hysterically.

"It's his knee," she said. "It's not a baby, it's the guy's knee."

Crisis averted. This guy's bony knee was positioned just perfectly against the window to make it look like a baby's head. We were pretty glad that we didn't call the police to report these reprobates with an infant in the front seat.

So what's the lesson here? The lesson is that sometimes you need to inspect the situation a little more deeply before you start jumping to conclusions.

And we see examples of that all the time in the financial world. Here's just two of them....

## "The market was up big but my account didn't grow much last year!"

At first blush, this might seem problematic. But it's important to take a step back and understand *why* your account didn't grow much. Is it because it's poorly allocated, or is the slow growth by design?

If you need that money in just a couple of years, you don't really want it to be behaving like the market. You want it to be invested more conservatively than that. So that lack of growth should be coming with a trade-off in the form of reduced volatility or downside. Looking a little deeper will help you determine if the lack of growth is intentional, or the result of incompetence.

## "My fees are too high—I found another advisor who will charge me less!"

Too often, people get too fixated on what fee their advisor is charging and don't pay enough attention to what they're actually getting in return.

Here's a good example to illustrate the point. Suppose you're looking for a landscaping company to take care of your yard. One company is going to charge $100/month, while the other one charges $135/month. Which one is better?

The answer seems obvious, right?

But what if we dig a little deeper and determine that the services aren't exactly the same? The first company is going to show up once a week and mow the grass. That's what you get for $100/month.

The second company is going to mow the grass, but they're also going to run the edger around the driveway and the sidewalk, weed eat along the fence around the back of the house, and pick up trash by the road. They're going to come by every other week in the fall and rake leaves. They'll re-seed in the winter and fertilize in the spring. And they'll come by twice a year and trim the hedges.

Suddenly that $135/month fee sounds pretty good compared to the guy who's mowing the yard and nothing else for $100.

So let's put that in a financial context. Suppose you have an advisor who says they'll manage your account for a 1% fee. Are they providing any other services in addition to managing that specific account?

What if somebody else is charging 1.25%, or maybe even 1.5% or 1.75%. Are those people also just managing the account? Or are they providing advice on how you should allocate your 401k? Helping you make decisions about Social Security or pensions? Helping you with cash management, long term care planning, or estate planning? Giving you tax advice?

There's not a specific menu of services that automatically justifies a certain fee. But it's important that you have an apples-to-apples discussion if you're comparing one fee/advisor to another.

So before you freak out about the baby in the front seat of your portfolio, dig a little bit deeper. If it's just a knee, there's no need to work yourself into a lather.

# 4 THE FINANCIAL SUITCASE

It's funny how your luggage evolves over the years.

I remember when I was in college, I'd go somewhere for the weekend and wouldn't even bother with luggage. I'd just throw a couple of pairs of underwear in the backseat, along with an extra shirt and pair of jeans, and all was well. If I really wanted to get fancy, I might use a grocery bag to tote this stuff around for a few days.

Then, as I came to accept the fact that I was considered an adult by most objective standards, I actually started using a more legitimate traveling bag of some sort. Still nothing fancy, but it technically qualified as luggage.

When we got married, my parents bought us one of those luggage sets with the three matching bags of various sizes that all fit inside of each other like Russian nesting dolls.

Then we had kids. Now when we travel, it looks like the Ringling Brothers have started using Southwest Airlines to move the circus from town to town.

Lilly ends up with a few bags, half of them filled with books, toys and stuffed animals. Amos usually gets a couple of bags to accommodate the diapers and piles of inevitable changes of clothes. Molly and I sometimes try to get all of our stuff in one bag, but that can be a challenge.

And then we each get a carry-on. Or as Jeff Foxworthy says, "Momma gets two carry-ons and I get to take whatever I can fit in my pockets."

But our current luggage situation is a helpful illustration for how I like to construct a retirement plan.

**1) Each bag has a job.**

I don't put my socks in the same bag as Lilly's stuffed animals. (She might move them there by the end of the trip, but that's never the original plan). I also don't stick Molly's curling iron in the same bag with my laptop.

There's a bag for adult clothes, another bag for kids' clothes. One bag for toiletries, another bag for laptop, iPad, and phone chargers.

The same thing needs to happen with your portfolio. Different accounts or different suitcases of money should have investments that are designed to accomplish a well-defined job for you.

**2) Your most vital items should go in your carry-on in case your luggage gets temporarily lost.**

Think about the things that you put in your carry-on bag. It's usually limited to the stuff you want to have with you on the plane, and the stuff that you absolutely have to have for your first day of the trip. That way if your luggage gets lost, you've bought yourself some time to get it back before your week is ruined.

In the financial world, everybody has some money that they can't afford to lose. And if you can't afford to temporarily lose it, you should have it in your financial carry-on. That is to say it should be sitting in accounts where the principal is protected from loss. But just like you can't pack for an entire trip in your carry-on bag, you can't overfund these accounts. Sure, it's nice that the principal is protected, but there are other jobs that those accounts can't accomplish for us.

**3) When your luggage does get lost, they'll get it back to you. Eventually.**

It could take just a few hours, or it could take a couple of days. But you'll eventually get your luggage back. And if you fly often enough, you're going to eventually experience lost luggage at some point.

Same thing with the market. If you invest in the market long enough, even if you're invested conservatively, you're going to take some hits. You'll sometimes lose your financial luggage. But that's ok, because you'll get it back. Eventually. So, if you packed your financial carry-on well enough, you don't have to panic.

## 4) Neatly and strategically folded clothes allow you to fit a lot more in your suitcase.

If you just ball up your clothes and toss them in the suitcase, you won't be able to get it zipped. But if they're neatly folded (or tightly rolled up, as Molly prefers to do it) you should be able to fit in everything you need without much trouble.

I still don't completely understand the physics of this. It's all the same amount of fabric, right? But a haphazardly collected pile of clothes simply takes up more space than a strategically folded stack.

The problem I see with a lot of financial suitcases is that they haven't been efficiently packed.

For instance, you might glance at the mutual fund options in your 401(k) for 45 seconds before you go cross-eyed and then rashly pick a few funds that don't seem to sound too bad. Then you have the account that you inherited from your parents and it's still invested in the same things they invested in 16 years ago. And then there's the 401(k) from your old job that you haven't even looked at since you left that company.

This is the financial equivalent of taking a pile of clothes out of your dresser, dropping that pile in your suitcase, and hoping you have everything you need for your trip. The reality is that you'll end up *without* a lot of financial tools that you do need, you will have packed a bunch of things that you *don't* need, and, to add insult to injury, your financial clothes will be really wrinkled when you arrive at your destination.

So what's the lesson here? First of all, don't use a grocery bag in lieu of a suitcase. You're better than that. Second, pay attention to the process next time you're packing for a trip. You might learn a little bit about retirement planning.

# 5 STUFF THAT DOESN'T WORK (IN LIFE AND MONEY)

There's lots of stuff in this world that just doesn't work, and that's not limited to the financial realm. Here are a few things that I've determined just don't work (some financial, some not):

**Thing That Doesn't Work #1: Arguing with people about political issues on Facebook**

Tell me how many times you've had this conversation with someone.

"Hey, so I heard that you switched party affiliations. What caused that change of heart?"

"Well, I've been engaged in a debate on Facebook with a girl I went to high school with. Haven't even seen her in probably 15 years, but she really made me think with her nine-paragraph response to something that I posted the other day. And then when she shared a 2013 article from Politico with me, I decided that now was the time to change my lifelong political ideology."

Remember all those times you've heard somebody say that? Me neither.

**Thing That Doesn't Work #2: The "Close Door" button on elevators**

They almost never work. It's usually a dummy button.

So what's going on here? Are the elevator manufacturers going out of their way to install an extra button that gives us the illusion of control?

Not exactly. In fact, the buttons *used* to work. Then along came the Americans with Disabilities Act and most places decided to disable the buttons to be in compliance with the law. Sure, they could give us some kind of signage to let us know that we're wasting our time pressing the button, but that seems like a lot of trouble.

## Thing That Doesn't Work #3: Timing the Market

About once a month, somebody will walk into my office, seemingly for no other reason than to tell me their story of how brilliantly they timed the market in 2000 or 2008 and how they got out at *just the right time* and avoided the crash.

This is a lot like somebody telling you about their recent trip to Vegas and how much money they made with their new blackjack strategy. Of course, they're forgetting to tell you about the previous four trips to Vegas where they lost all of their money but just couldn't stop playing and eventually found themselves pleading "GIVE ME MORE CREDIT" as they were whisked away to a dark room.

Is it possible that you can guess when the crash is coming and get out at just the right time? Sure, it's possible. Not highly likely, but within the realm of possibility. Then all you have to do is wait for the market to bottom out, then you come galloping back in on your steed, buy everything while it's deeply discounted and then ride it back to the top.

But that's the problem with successfully timing the market. You have to be right twice.

You have to not only get out at the right time, you also have to get back in at exactly the right time. And if you miss just a few days of a strong recovery and you get back in too late, you'll wipe out most of the money that you saved by avoiding the initial downturn.

To illustrate what I mean, here are some fun numbers, that I've borrowed (stolen?) from J.P. Morgan.

They did a study on the returns on $10,000 invested in the S&P 500 for 20 years—from January of 1995 through the end of 2014.

If you let the money ride untouched for the full 20 years, your $10,000 would have grown to $65,453. That's a 9.85% average annual return.

If you remove the gains from only the 10 best trading days during that 20 year period, you now have only $32,665. Half of your gains came during just *ten* trading days.

If you miss the 40 best trading days over a 20-year period, you actually have a negative return with your $10,000 now being worth $9,140.

So you can see what happens to a lot of people who successfully time the market and get out before the crash. While they're on a victory tour around the country club locker room celebrating their investing prowess, the market bounces back before they have a chance to go re-buy all of their stocks at bargain prices. By the time they re-invest, the market is pretty close to where it was when they got out, and they've accomplished almost nothing.

## Thing That Doesn't Work #4: Pick-up lines

"Hey Mom, how did you meet Dad?"

"Well, I was at this dumpy, crowded bar when this guy accidentally brushes up against me and then says 'Hey, are you an overdue library book?' And I looked at him with a puzzled look on my face and I said, 'No, I'm not, in fact, an overdue library book…why do you ask?' And he says, 'Because you have FINE written all over you!' And I blushed and giggled and he grabbed my hand and led me to the dance floor and I knew immediately that I wanted to bear his children."

Yep, that's usually how those pick-up lines work out. And they lived happily ever after.

# SECTION II:

## Financial Lessons from Famous Quotable People

# 6 A FOOL AND HIS MONEY

"A fool and his money are soon elected."

"I don't make jokes, I just watch the government and report the facts."

"If pro is the opposite of con, what's the opposite of Congress?"

If that sounds like the wit and wisdom of Mark Twain to you…well, that would be a good guess, but ultimately incorrect.

These are actually the witticisms of one of Twain's contemporaries, the waggish Will Rogers.

The overwhelming majority of Rogers' barbs were aimed at the politicians of his day, and though he uttered many of those quotes nearly 100 years ago, they're still remarkably apropos today.

But you could also assemble a well-conceived financial plan just by using some of his quotes as a guide. For instance…

**"Even if you're on the right track, you'll get run over if you just sit there."**

To a large extent, we strive for a certain level of "autopilot" in all of our retirement plans. Nobody wants to feel the need for constant changes to their plan in order to stay on track.

At the same time, we can't just put a plan into motion and then leave it alone for 30 years. Tweaks will need to be made along the way. The best example of this is the Constitution. If we were still rolling with the Constitution as it was originally drafted, with no amendments, we'd have quite a different country today. There would be no income tax (that's fun to dream about), women and black people wouldn't be voting, and we'd all be required to have soldiers living in our guest rooms.

We *would* still have the rule that you have to be born a citizen in order to be president. So, we wouldn't have to worry about a Schwarzenegger or Bieber presidency. The founding fathers were quite prescient on that one.

But in the financial context, the lesson is simple: just because you've arrived at the correct answer for today doesn't mean it will still be the correct answer at this time next year.

You should be constantly tweaking your plans as your circumstances in life change, continually reevaluating your risk tolerance and diversification, and making sure that each of your investments is accomplishing the mission that you assigned to it.

**"The difference between death and taxes is that death doesn't get worse every time Congress meets."**

I could easily spill a couple of barrels of ink just talking about taxes, but for now, just suffice it to say this: Taxes are going up in the future. There's really not a mathematical alternative.

I don't know how long the benevolent federal government will allow us to continue contributing to Roth IRAs before they decide that it creates too great a tax advantage for us down the road, but if you've been ignoring the Roth, you should probably think again, especially if you're still relatively young.

If you're under the age of, say, 45, there aren't many scenarios I can come up with where you should be contributing to a traditional IRA instead of a Roth. Between the ages of 45 and 60, it's much more of a case-by-case analysis. Over 60, you're often better off to contribute to the traditional instead of the Roth, but not always.

But if you believe that taxes are only going to increase for the remainder of your life, it doesn't make much sense to avoid paying taxes now so that you can instead pay them at some unknown (but almost certainly higher) rate down the road.

**"I'm not as interested in the return *on* my money as I am the return *of* my money."**

Or to put it in the words of one of my clients recently, "We're not that interested in growing our portfolio very much. At this point, our main focus is not losing what we have."

You need to be careful that you don't slip into this mindset too early in life when you still have a reasonably long timeline until retirement and several good earning years ahead of you. But at some point in your life, there will come a time when it's to shift your focus.

Over the years, I've seen too many people getting close to retirement (or already retired) who get caught up in an obsession of trying to maximize their investment returns. Once you reach this stage of your life, maximizing your returns becomes less crucial. You should instead be focused on preserving your wealth and using that wealth to create income.

**"Live in such a way that you would not be ashamed to sell your parrot to the town gossip."**

This has nothing to do with your retirement plan. But still good advice.

# 7 PRESIDENTIAL RETIREMENT PLANNING

It seems that most people who voted in the 2016 election weren't exactly voting *for* either of the presidential candidates. Most were either voting *against* Hillary Clinton (who seemed to be one of the most corrupt individuals in the history of American politics), or *against* Donald Trump (who seemed to be one of the most incompetent individuals in the history of American politics).

But there was a time in our country when the options on the ballot were a bit more palatable. So, let's hearken back to some presidents of the past, reflect on some of their wisdom, and then weave those quotes into retirement planning wisdom...

**"When only one side of a story is heard and often repeated, the human mind becomes impressed with it." – George Washington**

What's our financial connection here? Well, how often do we see the Wall Street machine create a narrative that becomes the accepted storyline? When the talking points have been repeated often enough, they eventually become the conventional wisdom.

One of the most the common Wall Street talking points is, "It's only a loss on paper. You haven't lost anything unless you sell."

Well, that's true if you're 35 years old and you don't *have* to sell anything. But what if you're 67 and you're retiring next year and you need to sell those shares of Proctor & Gamble to generate income? Suddenly that loss is a little more than a paper loss.

**"Trust but verify." – Ronald Reagan**

This can be a delicate balance to strike for a lot of people. Most people have one element mastered, but they struggle with the other one.

With some folks, trust is very difficult to earn. And in a couple of cases, I've actually told people that we shouldn't proceed with any planning because I can tell that they have trust issues and it's unlikely that we'll be able to accomplish anything.

For instance, I remember a lady who came to visit a couple of years ago. She wasn't very inclined to share much about her goals or dreams for retirement because she was too busy giving me the side-eye while she tried to discern how I was going to distract her with my left hand while stealing her wallet with my right. Needless to say, if there's not at least a reasonable expectation of trust from the very beginning, we're not going to get very far.

On the other hand, some people trust everything they're told way too readily and don't do a good job with the "verify" portion. A gentleman comes to mind who was ready to implement several different strategies before I'd even had a chance to describe any of them. I could tell he was way too eager, so I floated this test balloon:

"I think we should put half of your IRA into a variety of Middle Eastern currencies. The other half will be split between biopharma penny stocks and Guatemalan real estate."

I really thought he'd know I was joking. But he said, "You're the expert...let's do it!"

So I had to disabuse him of the notion that we'd be adding a Central American volcano to his portfolio. And then we had to have a little talk about the importance of understanding what he's doing before he does it.

**"Ask not what your country can do for you, ask what you can do for your country." – JFK**

What if all financial advisors said, "Ask not what this potential client can do for me, but what I can do for this potential client?"

If you're not already familiar with the concept of a fiduciary, it's something that you'll want to get acquainted with. A fiduciary is someone who's legally required to act in your best interest. That means an advisor who's a fiduciary would have to be able to prove in court that the advice they gave you was for your benefit, not to help them make a commission.

Here's a few types of people who are fiduciaries:

Attorneys
CPAs
Registered Investment Advisors
Realtors

And a few people who aren't:

Stockbrokers
Life insurance salesmen
Toyota dealers
Lou the butcher

Some people assume that their stockbroker is a fiduciary. But if his job is to sell stocks, he's really no different than the Toyota dealer whose job is to sell Toyotas…or the butcher whose job is to sell beef. If what you really need is a retirement income plan, a Honda Accord, and some fresh fish, then neither the stockbroker, the Toyota dealer, nor the butcher can really help you. They're just going to try and convince you that their product is what you *really* need.

Does that mean that all attorneys and investment advisors are perfect fits for you? No. Nor does it mean that the guy trying to sell you a life insurance policy is a charlatan. But if you'll take a moment to understand how people are compensated, you'll have a better understanding of how to filter the advice they give you.

# 8 YOGISMS

"Nobody goes there nowadays, it's too crowded."

I don't know what Yogi Berra was referencing when he dropped that quip, but I can only assume he was talking about Brigs at the Park on Highway 55 in Durham. Nobody even thinks about going there after church on Sunday because it's just too crowded.

But Yogi's quotes are good for more than just brunch advice. We can actually extract a lot of retirement planning wisdom from some of the things he said. Let's break down a few classic Yogi-isms and find the financial planning wisdom within…

**"I never said most of the things I said."**

Have you ever had an experience where you thought you were buying something with a particular feature or benefit, but then down the road you discover that everything you remember from the sales pitch isn't actually true?

Cable companies are the worst examples of this. The sales guy will promise you literally anything just to get the sale made. Then when the tech guy shows up to install everything, you suddenly find out that the laws of physics don't mesh with what the sales guy told you.

"They said the TV would be able to read your brainwaves and you could change the channel just by thinking about it and you don't even have to use the remote? No ma'am, we can't actually do that."

But good luck getting anyone at the cable company to acknowledge the fact that you were led astray.

"Oh, Ted told you that? He's not with the company anymore." Or in other words, "We never said most of the things we said."

In the financial world, this confusion usually manifests itself in the form of investment projections. It's important to understand the difference between something that's contractually guaranteed to happen and something that *could* happen. If you're being given a sales pitch for a particular product, there's a good chance that a lot of time will be spent on what *could* happen. Be sure you have a clear understanding of what's being *promised*, as opposed to what's being *projected*.

## "A nickel ain't worth a dime anymore."

Well Yogi, I'm not positive that a nickel was *ever* worth a dime, if we're being technical. But your point is understood. Inflation can really take a toll on the buying power of a dollar.

When you think about the fact that inflation hums along at a rate somewhere between 2.25-to-3% per year (depending on which statistician you ask), that metric by itself doesn't seem all that daunting.

But once you start adding up the cumulative effect of inflation over the course of a 30-year retirement, suddenly the situation appears to be a bit more daunting. If you're retiring at 63 and you want to spend $8,000 every month, that means you're going to spend $16,000 each month when you're 85, if you want to have the same buying power.

Most people understand the concept of inflation, but haven't really stopped to assess just how much it needs to be factored into their retirement income planning.

Just like you occasionally get a raise at work (maybe even on an annual basis, depending on the company), you need to be able to give yourself a raise in retirement.

## "It's like déjà vu all over again."

The cycles in the stock market usually look pretty similar. Things are going well and everybody is buying, then there's a crash or a correction, and suddenly everybody is panicking and selling. Nobody can predict *when* these things are going to happen, but the way that people behave during these periods is always startlingly predictable.

And everybody always thinks they learned their lesson from the last crash…until we get a few years down the road and suddenly everybody behaves the same way they did during the last crash.

I spend a decent portion of my week talking to other advisors around the country, and the consensus is that most of them aren't bringing on nearly as many new clients as they were five or six years ago. The reason for that is five or six years ago, the crash of 2008 was still very fresh in everyone's mind, and they recognized the need for help with their retirement planning.

As I write this in the spring of 2017, it's almost as if nobody remembers that crash. Most people don't perceive the need for any help or guidance. The average investor is quite content with the performance of his 401k, and assumes that he's finally gotten the hang of this game called investing. The reality, of course, is that a bull market has the power to cover up a lot of mistakes, so you don't recognize the things you're doing wrong.

But then the market crash will come and it will be déjà vu all over again.

The key, as always, is having a solid plan in place that addresses all of these issues and more—inflation, market volatility, tax efficiency, predictable income, etc.

Because, as Yogi said, "If you don't know where you're going, you might wind up some place else."

# 9 UNCOMMON SENSE

Many good quotes about common sense have been uttered over the centuries...

"Common sense in an uncommon degree is what the world calls wisdom." – Samuel Taylor Coleridge

"Common sense is not so common." – Voltaire

"Common sense is the most widely shared commodity in the world, for every man is convinced that he is well supplied with it." – Descartes

"Common sense is genius dressed in its working clothes." – Ralph Waldo Emerson

The financial world is riddled with opportunities for people to violate some basic principles of common sense. Let's explore a couple of them.

**Buy Low and Sell High**

Pretty obvious, right? I've never encountered a single person who disagrees with the wisdom of this common sense investing principle.

And yet, when I examine investing behavior, I constantly see people in violation of it.

Here's the perfect example. I once met with a fellow who walked in the office with a portfolio valued at roughly $750,000. Before the 2008 financial crisis, he had close to $1.3 million. But after the crash, when he saw his account balance dropped by about 40%, he panicked, pulled his money out of the market, and stuck it in a money market account where he's been making 1% ever since.

Obviously, he sold low. (You might recall that you're supposed to sell *high*).

But that's not the end of it. He walked in my office saying that he was tired of having his money sitting in cash earning 1% interest and he'd like to get back in the market.

At the time of this conversation, we'd been hitting a new all-time high in the market every week.

So, he *sold low*, camped out in cash for several years, and now he wanted to *buy high*. The exact opposite of what you're supposed to be doing, on both fronts!

And while it's easy to scoff at his extreme violation of the "buy low, sell high" principle, it's not like he's the only person that I've seen who's guilty of this. I see it all the time—maybe not to that extreme, but I see some version of that story at least once a month.

Buy low, sell high. Common sense that isn't so common.

## Don't Pay More in Taxes Than You Have To

There are varying levels with which people revile taxes.

At one end of the spectrum, you have people who say things like, "Well, I don't like paying taxes, but I try to be conscious of the government services that I benefit from and that usually makes me feel better."

At the other end, you have the people who are ready to secede from the union at the mere mention of the IRS.

But there's *nobody* who's voluntarily signing up to send more money to the government than they're required to send because they feel that the folks in Washington are a beacon of efficiency and virtue and they want to help them fund a few more studies about the effects of cow flatulence on the environment.

Well, I shouldn't say *nobody*. There's probably somebody in Carrboro who can't get enough of the federal government constantly expanding and wants

38

to contribute every penny he can to that enterprise. But other than that one guy, then "nobody" is probably a safe word to use here.

And yet I frequently see people paying more in taxes than they have to.

Sometimes it's just laziness when it comes to tax preparation—like taking the standard deduction when you could itemize your deductions and be much better off.

But more often, it's a problem of tax planning. Most of your tax mistakes aren't going to occur when you're doing your taxes every spring. It's the opportunities that you miss *now* to save yourself some money five years down the road.

Here's one example of tax planning. Consider the decision about whether you should contribute to a traditional IRA or a Roth IRA. With the traditional IRA, you get a tax deduction in the year that you make the contribution, but all of the growth in that account is eventually going to be taxed. With the Roth IRA, you don't get a deduction for making the contribution, but all of the growth is tax-free. Deciding which type of account to contribute to is going to be determined by your current tax bracket, your projected tax bracket in retirement, your timeline for investing the money, and a host of other considerations.

Tax planning rarely involves clear black and white decisions, but usually involves a lot of nuance and multi-faceted considerations. So, it's not always simple, but it's important.

So do some planning and don't pay more than you have to. Unless you're really into cow flatulence.

# SECTION III:

# Financial Lessons from Classic TV

# 10 THE POOR MOUNTAINEER

Everybody knows the story of Jed Clampett. Poor mountaineer, barely kept his family fed. But then he struck oil in his backyard in the Ozarks, became an overnight millionaire and moved to Beverly Hills.

Obviously, in Uncle Jed's case, he didn't quite know how to handle those riches. He ended up with a nice mansion and a cement pond in the backyard, but he struggled to navigate the puzzling social morays of Beverly Hills. Neighbors always seemed annoyed, for some reason, when he pulled out his shotgun to eliminate any vermin who might be patrolling the neighborhood.

The closest real-life situation I've heard about wasn't a client of mine, but a client of one of my friends in Texas. She has a client who lives about 30 miles outside of San Antonio who's been a chicken farmer his whole life. They discovered oil on his land and he now gets a royalty check for more than a million dollars every month. Not every year…every month. But all he really cares about in life is being a chicken farmer, so he often doesn't even think to cash the checks. He'll walk around with a crumpled-up million-dollar check in his pocket for weeks at a time.

While I haven't encountered any situations quite like this myself, I've often seen lump sums of money lead to uncomfortable situations when people aren't getting the proper guidance.

It could be an inheritance that you didn't necessarily anticipate. Maybe you're expecting to get *something* from your parents (like maybe the house and whatever happens to be in their checking account on the day they die). But then you're completely taken by surprise when you find out there's also

43

a $450,000 IRA and a $100,000 life insurance payout that's now headed your way.

For other people, it's a pension buyout. Maybe you've never done a great job of saving over the years, knowing that you'd have a sizeable pension to help carry you through retirement. But then one day you find out that instead of $2500/month for the rest of your life, you'll instead be getting a $385,000 lump sum buyout, which you now have to figure out how to invest in such a way that it makes up for the fact that you no longer have that pension check hitting the bank account every month.

Or maybe you actually did strike oil in the backyard. I guess that could happen.

Whatever the case may be, anytime you end up with a lump sum (expected or unexpected), you need to be sure you're getting proper guidance. Here's one example of a time when I saw someone get bad advice:

A BCBSNC employee was given the option of keeping her pension or receiving a pension buyout. She could retire at 62 and have a monthly pension income of just over $3,000/month, or she could take a lump sum of $550,000.

She ended up talking to an "advisor" whose only real interest was selling her an annuity, so he convinced her to take the lump sum (a decision she had to make on a short deadline) while he went to look for an annuity that would give her a lifetime income that would "blow away" her pension. So, she made the irreversible decision of electing the lump sum. Now the annuity salesman tells her that there's actually not an annuity that will take her lump sum and give her an income that's bigger than what her pension would have been. But if she'll just plop the $550,000 into the annuity and wait for six years, well *then* it will give her an income that will blow away her pension.

Of course, she wasn't happy with this option and ended up in my office looking for a better solution. We found a better solution than what he was offering (which did involve an annuity, but only using about $175,000 of that $550,000…with the rest of the money invested in the market). But the fact of the matter is that she would have ultimately been better off to have just taken the pension. Unfortunately, it was too late to make that decision by the time she made it to my office, so we just had to make the best of the situation at that point.

So a lump sum is nothing to be scared of, but if you make a few wrong turns, you could easily end up as a hillbilly in a fancy neighborhood trying to figure out why you don't fit in. (Metaphorically, of course).

While we're on the subject, here's some Uncle Jed trivia. Most people know that Buddy Ebsen was originally supposed to play the Tin Man in the Wizard of Oz, but he had an allergic reaction to the aluminum dust from the costume and ended up in the hospital. Jack Haley came in and took over the role, and he's the one we know as the Tin Man today.

However, most people aren't aware that Buddy Ebsen still contributed to the film. They'd already filmed some scenes with him as the Tin Man, and while they had to reshoot all of those scenes with Jack Haley, they didn't want to scrap the soundtrack. So, when you hear Dorothy, the Scarecrow and the Tin Man harmonizing in "We're Off to See the Wizard," that's actually Uncle Jed's voice as the Tin Man.

This piece of trivia has very little to do with your retirement planning, but it's interesting nonetheless.

So what's the lesson we learn from Uncle Jed? If you've never been financially savvy, don't make decisions too hastily whenever you encounter a lump sum decision or a financial windfall of some kind. Seek good guidance, take your time, and be sure you understand all of your options.

# 11 THOSE WERE THE DAYS

To quote Archie and Edith, "Mister, we could use a man like Herbert Hoover again."

Actually, I have no idea if that's true. I'm guessing it's not. Some historians say that he was one of the worst presidents. Others say he was simply one of the unluckiest.

But we're not here to reflect on the tenure of the first president born west of the Mississippi. (There's some presidential trivia you can use to impress your friends at dinner parties). We're here to talk about the good ol' days.

I'll admit that I'm as guilty as anyone of sometimes thinking we'd be better off with the way things used to be, financially speaking. Every month when I look through our household budget, I can only shake my head at the amount of money that gets spent on things that weren't household expenses when I was a kid (either because they didn't exist, or because it just wasn't something that most people spent money on). For example:

- Gym membership
- Cell phones
- Satellite/cable TV
- Netflix/Hulu/Amazon Prime Video
- Internet
- Sponsored kids in Kenya (I'm sure Kenyans existed when I was a kid, but

to my knowledge, they didn't have so many programs that made it so easy to send money to them)

In our household, that list alone represents $664 every month to pay for things that weren't around in the good ol' days.

I hear a lot of wistfulness for the good ol' days among my clients too. But their complaints tend to revolve more around the current investing environment and general retirement planning landscape.

For example, the disappearance of pensions is a sore spot for many. People love to cite the fact that their mom is 92 and never saved much for retirement, but she's in fine shape financially because she's still living off Dad's pension.

Another complaint is interest rates. Most people like that 3.25% interest rate on their mortgage, but that satisfaction seems to be offset by the paltry 0.95% they're earning with their money market account.

And then there's inflation. "We paid less for our first house than we did for the car we just bought!" Apparently, the car dealerships print that out on a little card and give it to every car buyer over the age of 65 right before they drive off the lot, because I hear that one all the time.

So let's rewind a couple of generations and talk about retirement in the good ol' days. It usually looked something like this...

It's 1975. Grandad retires at age 65 after a 42-year career at the textile mill, where they give him a gold watch and a pension. Combining that pension with Social Security for him and Grandma, they have a monthly income of $1,850, which sounds like the poverty line, but is actually equivalent to $8,250 in today's money. They haven't had any debt since the first year of the Eisenhower administration, and that $1,850 is more than they can spend every month.

Grandad never saved a ton of money, but he does have $45,000 in a CD that's paying him 10.25% interest. So, there's another $4600/year (or nearly $21,000 in today's dollars), which they also don't need.

And by the way, life expectancy is 72 years, so the chances of living long enough to end up in a nursing home are slim.

If I'm their financial advisor in 1975, my job is easy. My advice would sound something like this:

"Keep spending money on the same stuff you've always spent money on, splurge a little bit because you can, and leave an inheritance to the kids. Now, here's a little parting gift for you, it's a brand-new craze called the 'mood ring.' Hold on to it because it will probably be worth a lot someday."

Those were the days.

Now compare that to the current environment...

- Life expectancies continue to increase, so the chances of a nursing home stay for any given individual are higher than ever.
- Our rapidly increasing national debt means that we'll almost certainly be seeing an increase in both tax rates and inflation down the road.
- CDs and money markets are paying basically nothing.
- Markets are more volatile than they've ever been.
- Pensions are quickly becoming extinct.
- Robin Williams and Princess Di are dead, but O.J. Simpson and Keith Richards are somehow still alive.

It's a crazy, unexplainable world out there, and if retirement is on the horizon for you, you have a long list of challenging issues to address. Just because Grandad was able to do it all without professional help doesn't mean you should try to do the same.

Get some help and you'll be more likely to end up with what Archie would call "a happy frame of mood."

# 12 THE CURMUDGEON

Sometimes, you're surprised when you find out what TV characters were like in real life. Like Aunt Bee, for example. If you only knew her from *Andy Griffith* episodes, you'd assume that Frances Bavier was exactly the same person in real life.

Not even close. In reality, she was incredibly unpleasant to be around. First of all, she felt that her New York City acting pedigree wasn't being fully utilized and that her dramatic talents were being overlooked on the show. She was easily offended during filming and everybody on the production staff always walked on eggshells around her. In her later years, she moved to Siler City where she died as a recluse with 14 cats.

But on the other hand, some actors are *exactly* who you'd expect them to be in real life. William Frawley, known by most as Fred Mertz on *I Love Lucy*, fits that bill.

He was a crotchety curmudgeon on the show, and apparently even more cantankerous in real life. His career was filled with spats with producers, and he was once fired for punching another actor in the nose. When Desi Arnaz called him to offer him the job of playing Fred, Desi told William that he'd be on a short a leash. He behaved well enough to avoid being written out of the show, but didn't exactly make a lot of friends during the show's six seasons. (And apparently Fred and Ethel despised each other in real life).

But it's the character of Fred Mertz, not the actor William Frawley, that we want to focus on here.

Fred was a tightwad. A cheapskate. Parsimonious. Niggardly. Miserly. Penurious. Use whatever vocabulary word you want, but he wouldn't spend money on anything. Always taking the cheapest way out. Complaining about every penny he had to spend on anything. It was probably the most defining element of his character.

And while a lot of people don't realize it, they actually *become* Fred Mertz once they retire.

That happens because they don't have an income plan. See, when you're working, you don't have any trouble spending money. You spend money with confidence because you're confident that you'll get a paycheck next month to replenish the money that you just spent. But that mental paradigm changes when you shift from earning a paycheck to now living off your savings.

If you don't have an income plan in retirement, it's hard to spend with confidence. Without an income plan, you just have a big pile of money sitting there. And you're hoping that you can take a small enough chunk of money out of that pile each month so that you don't have to worry about running out.

I've seen a lot of people who actually have plenty of money saved for retirement—more than enough to give them the lifestyle that they want for the rest of their lives. But because they're worried about eventually running out, they don't pay themselves as much as they could. Which means not taking the trips that they want to take, or not giving as much to the church as they want to, or not taking the family out to eat, even though they really want to.

Or maybe they do actually spend money on all of those things, but they don't fully enjoy it because they're worried about the price tag. Something in the back of their mind is telling them that they're spending too much.

An income plan tells you where the paychecks are going to come from, not just next month, but for the rest of your life. And once you see it on paper, and see how you need to invest in order to make the income plan work, you wouldn't believe the confidence that you'll have.

So get an income plan and spend with confidence. Don't be Fred. Nobody really liked him.

# 13 LITTLE BUDDY

You don't have to look very hard to find a lot of fun conspiracy theories about *Gilligan's Island*.

One theory is that the whole ordeal was perpetrated by the Howells. Their businesses were collapsing so they decided to create a new world for themselves. They specifically selected certain people to end up on this boat with them in the middle of nowhere. The Professor was essentially MacGyver, with his ability to make anything out of random spare parts. Ginger and Mary Ann were eye candy for Mr. Howell. The Skipper was there for manual labor for Mrs. Howell. And Gilligan is the buffoon who constantly ruins the plans to get off the island, thus solidifying the Howell's reign forever.

After assembling their dream team, all they had to do was check the weather reports and head out for their boat ride on a day when they knew they were likely to get swept away by a storm.

The best support for this theory is the fact that the Howells are wearing different clothes almost every episode. Why would somebody bring so much luggage for a three-hour tour? Maybe because they knew it was actually going to be 98 episodes instead of just three hours?

Another theory is that this was a drug deal that hit a few snags. Thurston Howell was a drug dealer to the rich and famous on his way to rendezvous with a supplier in the South Pacific. That would explain his suitcase full of cash.

The Professor had seven college degrees, but Howell only needed him for his chemistry knowledge. Gotta have somebody to check the quality of the merchandise.

Ginger was a movie star. Obviously, a customer of Howell's. And Mary Ann was either an unsuspecting tourist, or a narc who was hot on Howell's trail.

Finally, there's one conspiracy theory that's actually true...or mostly true. The theory posits that the island is hell, with each of the characters representing the seven deadly sins. Mr. Howell is obviously greed. Mrs. Howell represents gluttony. Ginger is lust. Mary Ann, always jealous of Ginger, represents envy. The Professor, with all of his fancy book learnin', represents pride. The Skipper is wrath. And Gilligan embodies sloth.

Years after the show went off the air, Sherwood Schwartz, the show's creator, wrote in his book that this last theory is actually true. Not the part about the island being hell, but the fact that each of the characters was based on one of the seven deadly sins.

None of these theories have anything to do with my main point. I really just wanted to talk about Gilligan, but couldn't help wandering down this conspiracy theory rabbit trail.

In any event, forget about the seven deadly sins. Instead, think about Gilligan the way that most people remember him. He was so lovable. Innocent, naïve, and really had the best of intentions. But at the same time, he also had some really bad luck and an accident-prone way of clumsily stumbling through life.

I recently met somebody who was in the same boat. (Pun intended). He was a real-life Gilligan.

Super nice guy. He sees the good in everyone. Even if you've only known him for five minutes, he acts like you've been best friends for 35 years. He stops to give money to every panhandler he sees and can't help but pick up the phone to make a donation to the ASPCA when he sees the commercial with the abandoned puppies.

And when it came to his investing life, he was a toxic combination of bad luck and terrible decision-making. When he got divorced several years ago, his ex-wife's legal team ran circles around his attorney. He'd invested some money in his brother-in-law's business about a decade ago—that was

54

$50,000 that evaporated almost immediately. His cat has a rare blood disease that requires a specialized treatment costing several thousand dollars a year.

After the market crashed in 2008, he decided to get out of stocks altogether, and he never got back in. So, he took all of those losses, sold at the very bottom, and then parked himself in cash and didn't experience the many years of bull markets that followed.

And the crowning blow—he'd had a "financial advisor" who swindled him out of tens of thousands of dollars about 15 years ago. That guy is now in jail, but our real-life Gilligan never got his money back.

The sad thing about *Gilligan's Island* was that the show ended with everybody still stuck on the island. When the third season of the show ended, a fourth season was expected. So, the last episode of season three ended just like all of the other episodes, with the bubble-headed Gilligan ruining everyone's chance to get off the island. But then season four was abruptly cancelled, and Gilligan and his buddies were stranded forever.

For our real-life Gilligan, fortunately, there was hope. It took several months of helping him get organized, rectifying some old tax mistakes to pacify the IRS, putting together a plan that had him putting his money into legitimate investments instead of fantastical family businesses or too-good-to-be-true scams.

It certainly wasn't an overnight fix. After decades of bad decisions that had him financially marooned on a deserted island, we weren't going to be able to rescue him with the snap of a finger. But with a logical course and a clear destination, he's in a much better position than he used to be, and improving more every month.

Here's the point. For some people, once they decide that they're a financial Gilligan, they just give up and assume they'll be stuck on this island forever. They assume that they'll be working until they're 78, then living in poverty for the rest of their lives after that. But I've never actually found a case that's completely hopeless. A little planning can make up for a lot of past mistakes.

And it's funny how it usually unfolds. When you take charge of your own situation, instead of just being depressed about your situation, that's when your ship usually comes in.

# SECTION IV:

# Financial Lessons from People I've Met

# 14 GREAT EXPECTATIONS

I recently stumbled across some kind of dating advice radio show. I have no idea what it was or how I came across it. The first caller I heard opined that he couldn't ever get dates with women that he was interested in. He always got a lot of interest from women, he said, but only from girls that he wasn't attracted to.

The host asked him to describe the type of woman that he was attracted to.

"Well, you know, a really pretty face and a great body. But it's not all about looks, I also place a lot of emphasis on intelligence and a good sense of humor too."

"Terrific criteria," the host commended. "You've just described a '10.' Now, how would you describe yourself?"

The caller tried hard to sell himself. But the host kept interrupting him to press for more information on several different topics until we had a pretty good profile of this guy: an unemployed former video game store cashier in his late 30s with a rapidly receding hairline and a rapidly expanding waistline. He was a dog lover, so that was one mark in his favor, I guess.

"You've just described yourself as a three," the host said. "A four at best. And you're trying to find a girl that's a 10. This is a simple case of you needing to lower your standards."

Brutal advice. But a good lesson in managing your expectations. And it reminds me of a couple I visited with several years ago.

They had about $800,000 in their retirement accounts and wanted to be sure they could spend about $6,000 every month in retirement, while still leaving something to the kids. This seemed like it would be relatively easy to achieve, so I retreated to my financial laboratory and got to work on a plan for them.

We got together a week later to lay it all out. I showed them a plan where they actually ended up with a little *more* than their $6,000 monthly goal, and would still be able to pass $200,000 *apiece* to their two sons. Another successful day of retirement planning wizardry!

Except she was less than enthralled.

"Wait a minute. We have $800,000 now. And you're telling me that we'll only be able to pass HALF of that amount down to the boys? How can we have less money when we die than we have now?"

I consider myself fortunate to be here today telling you this story, because I'm still surprised that the insanity of this comment didn't cause my head to explode and splatter brains all over the wall in my office.

"Of *course* you'll have less money when you die! You will have been taking money *out* of your accounts for 25 to 30 years to meet your income needs!"

I'm actually not sure if I said that out loud or just said it to myself. I was a little awestruck by her expectations that she clearly thought were reasonable. But they weren't.

Apparently, when she'd said in our first meeting that they wanted to leave "something" to the boys, her definition of "something" varied considerably from mine. A failure on my part to not clarify expectations from the very beginning.

And while this is probably an extreme example of expectations run amok, unrealistic expectations actually aren't that uncommon when it comes to people and their money. For some folks, it's an unrealistic notion of how much risk they can afford to take with their retirement dollars. For others, it's an unreasonable percentage that they want to withdraw from their savings each year. And for some, it's an unrealistic notion of when they can actually retire.

But we also find out-of-whack expectations at the other end of the spectrum. These are the people who are in much better financial shape than they think, and they're convinced that they're going to have to work until another 12 years, even though they could have comfortably retired four years ago.

These people are the inverse of the radio caller we discussed earlier. They're like the "ten" woman who doesn't know how spectacular she is, so she always ends up dating losers.

So it's important to have a clear picture of what's realistic and what's not when it comes to your retirement planning. If you're a *four* looking for a *ten*, you probably won't get a lot of dates. But if you're a *ten*, then you should probably stop dating members of the opposite sex who can't seem to hold down a job for more than four months or keep their nose hairs trimmed to an acceptable length.

# 15 THE MEDIA OBSESSION

Mark Twain said, "If you don't read the newspaper, you're uninformed. If you do read the newspaper, you're mis-informed."

Swap out "read the newspaper" for "watch cable news" and that's still a startlingly accurate assessment more than 100 years after he said it.

Consider the following comments that clients emailed to me within mere days of each other. This was during the first month of Donald Trump's presidency:

1) "I may be more nervous than some people; I'm a serious newshound. However, I'm getting extremely cold feet about the political situation. I know stocks continue to go up on business' reaction to Trump's policies, but I simply can't imagine that his craziness isn't going to catch up with him, and us."

2) "I'd wanted to keep my accounts conservative until after the election, because I thought Hillary was going to win and I assumed the market would tank. But I have to say I'm PUMPED about President Trump and wondering if it's time to get more aggressive. I think we're going to see a terrific 3-4 years in the market. Would you agree?"

3) "Why is the market still going up? Do people not see what's happening in our country? There's a new protest or riot every day. I'm going to stop watching the news and start watching *The Bachelor* instead. I might end up dumber, but at least I'll be able to sleep at night."

Those comments represent some different worldviews, but all three of these folks have one thing in common—they consume a lot of news.

Think back to the way that you got your news a few decades ago. You had the morning newspaper and the evening news.

People actually paid significant sums of money to advertise in the newspaper, which meant newspapers were able to actually pay reporters and practice journalism. The evening news lasted a half hour and was designed to inform you about the major stories happening both nationally and internationally.

These methods weren't perfect (clearly Mark Twain had some issues with his local newspaper), but there were some clear advantages to living in a time like that when you compare it to our media landscape today.

Look at our current situation. Nobody reads an actual, tangible newspaper anymore. As everything moved online, less credible news outlets suddenly started being viewed as having the same credibility as the well-established journalistic beacons of the past. Because the barrier to entry in the media world was now so much lower (it's much easier and cheaper to launch a website than it is to print a newspaper), we ended up with an ever-increasing number of "news outlets." Because of the increased supply of media, it became much harder for the outfits practicing actual journalism to find the ad revenue they needed, which resulted in cutting staff (meaning fewer journalists) and more salacious headlines and stories to increase page views (meaning less commitment to actual journalism).

The evening news, which used to last a half hour, now runs 24 hours a day, on three different cable networks. Unfortunately, there's just not that much news worth reporting, so we end up with four-person panels debating a topic to death and "experts" from different sides of the aisle yelling at each other until we're all convinced that there will be a civil war commencing tomorrow afternoon.

So what we're left with is a lot of hysteria. No matter who lives in the White House or who controls Congress at any given moment, you'll find that most people either live in a state of intense fear that the republic is coming to an end or a state of euphoria based on the belief that the current leadership is leading us to the promised land. If you were in a state of euphoria a couple of years ago, you're probably catatonic right now. And vice versa.

All of these emotions are reflected in the investment world. Intense fear and unmitigated euphoria are both feelings that you shouldn't allow to dictate your investment decisions.

Back to our three clients that we mentioned earlier. The good news in all three of those cases is that they have an advisor—me—to keep them from making any hasty decisions about anything. But for every investor who has a coach to prevent them from leaping off a tall building, there's probably six or seven more who don't have any guidance and end up making hasty decisions. That's one of the main reasons that the market can be so volatile. The highs are higher than they should be and the lows are lower than they have to be.

I don't advocate living in a bunker and ignoring current events, but be careful how much you allow the media to dictate your emotional state. It's not good for your mental health or your portfolio.

# 16 THE SECOND OPINION

Thankfully, they were both smart. He was a microbiologist; she was an attorney.

They liked their financial advisor and said he'd put together a comprehensive financial plan for them. They just wanted to do their due diligence and get a second opinion before implementing it.

So we dove right in and I started flipping through the 43-page document. I tried to maintain my composure as long as I could, but I couldn't hold my tongue for very long.

"This is BALDERDASH!"

I'm pretty sure it's the only time I've ever used the word "balderdash" in regular conversation. I immediately wondered if I'd been a little too brash, until they both smirked a little bit.

"We wondered if that might be the case. It seemed a little too good to be true."

Thankfully, they were astute enough to come get a second opinion. After all, you don't get jobs in micro biologizing and lawyering without a relatively high level of intelligence.

But a lot of people don't bother with the second opinion, which concerns me.

The truth was that their "advisor" wasn't even someone they'd met in person. The company that administers his 401(k) had said, "Hey, were you aware that we provide free financial advice to highly compensated employees like you?" Which is code for, "Hey, we'd like to get our hands on *all* of your money, instead of only having the money that's in your 401(k), so if we overwhelm you with a document that looks impressive even though it's actually meaningless, maybe you'll move all of your life savings over to our company, yes?"

So here we had a *salesperson* masquerading as an *advisor*. Might it be possible that his plan was not actually a plan at all?

As I started to explore the stack of paper, I found that out of the 43 pages, 35 of them were boiler plate filler that had nothing to do with their specific case. But, in fairness, at least the information contained in these 35 pages was accurate. The eight pages that addressed their personal details didn't hold up so well.

The problems with this plan included, but were not limited to:

1) The plan assumed a rate of inflation of 1%. Nope, that should be more like 3%. So, their income needs later in life were going to be much higher than the plan projected.

2) The plan assumed a cost of living raise on their Social Security of 2.5% per year. Nope, that should be more like 1%. So, their Social Security income later in life was projected to be much higher than it actually will be.

3) In the first five years of retirement, he projected that they'd withdraw 15% of their portfolio each year! If you're keeping score at home, that withdrawal rate is about as sustainable as pouring yourself a nice, tall glass of orange juice every morning and hoping that the half gallon carton you bought last week is going to last you for a year before it runs out of juice. But this insane withdrawal rate actually worked out just fine in his fantasy world, because he also projected that they were going to earn 17% on their investments each year. In other words, a magical orange juice fairy was going to refill the carton every night to be sure that it lasts forever.

I'm pretty sure this was the part where I felt the "balderdash" word roll off my tongue.

After combing through this dumpster fire of a "plan," I felt compelled to find out more about the advisor who had constructed it. I looked him up and discovered the least surprising news of the day—the fact that he'd filed personal bankruptcy a few years earlier.

Well, of course he had. Because he doesn't understand how math works.

Now, if they'd implemented this plan, it's not as if this advisor would have disappeared to Belize with their money. But they would have been operating under the assumption that they were in much better shape than they actually were. After some real analysis, we determined that, in order to have the retirement lifestyle that they wanted, they needed to work about two years longer than this plan had indicated that they should.

This wasn't really bad news to them. They were fine with working the extra two years, they just wanted to know the truth and wanted to know what they needed to do.

Here's the point. Most of these "plans" that get handed out by big brokerage firms don't involve any actual planning. It's all based on formulaic, cookie-cutter assumptions that have nothing to do with the specifics of your life. And, as we saw in this particular case, they're often riddled with ridiculous assumptions.

When you're looking for a financial advisor, you want someone who can apply wisdom to your situation, not just somebody who can punch a few numbers into a software program.

If the financial advice you've gotten isn't tailored to the specific details of your life, get a second opinion. That's what smart people do.

# 17 RICH PEOPLE

Rich people always get blamed for stuff that isn't their fault. Or, depending on who you ask, they always get away with everything that *is* their fault while the little man takes the blame.

And to make things even more complicated, you'll also find a lot of conflicting definitions about who's rich and who isn't.

Some people say that you can identify a rich person by the six-figure income. Others would say it's the seven-figure net worth. Some would gauge your wealth by the size of your home, the quality of your car, or the person who designed your clothes.

I've been to Kenya and they use different metrics there. It usually involves donkeys. To quote my friend David Muchai, a lifelong citizen of Kenya:

"Look at this man over here. He has two donkeys. He is very rich."

Or later: "That man has one donkey. He is doing pretty well."

And finally: "Look at that man pulling his cart. He is poor. He doesn't have a donkey. He is using human donkey."

So it's hard to get a consensus on who's rich and who isn't. Perhaps it's helpful to clarify what a "rich" person looks like when it comes to retirement planning. Consider the following two clients that I've worked with for several years:

**Client #1:** Husband and wife combined make about $85,000/year. They have just over $350,000 in savings and they plan to retire in the next 3-4 years when they both turn 66. They'll need an income of about $5,000/month to maintain their lifestyle and also enjoy the traveling that they want to do once they retire.

**Client #2:** Husband makes about $250,000/year, wife doesn't work. They have more than $2 million in savings. He's 58 and wants to retire at 60. To achieve their desired lifestyle, they'll need an income of about $14,000/month, plus another $10,000/year for travel.

So which of these clients is wealthy?

Client #1 is, by far, the wealthier of the two.

Contrary to popular thinking, I don't measure a person's wealth by how much money they have or how much they make. It has much more to do with the ratio of their assets to their spending.

Let's think about situation #1. They're going to retire at full retirement age for Social Security. They both earn an income (and they both have for 40+ years), meaning they'll both have a decent Social Security benefit whenever they start it. In fact, their combined Social Security benefits will account for $4,350 in monthly income.

That means we'll need an additional $650/month to meet their needs. They could create that income by drawing down about 2.2% of their portfolio each year. That's very realistic and easy to achieve. They could actually retire a year earlier than they planned and be just fine.

On the other hand, the gaudy salary and account balance touted by Client #2 doesn't mean that they're in great shape. He wants to retire at 60, which is two years before he can start Social Security. That means that *all* of their income in the first couple of years will need to come from savings.

This means a drawdown rate of 8.9% in the first couple of years. Completely unsustainable!

We also have a catch-22 with Social Security. If we start it at age 62, it will at least partially stop the bleeding on their portfolio, because now we won't have to keep taking out 8.9% every year to create the income that they want. But we'd still need more than 6%, which is still way too much.

Suppose we wait to start Social Security at a later date. Sure, we'll have a larger benefit, but that also means more years of drawing down that portfolio at a rate of 8.9%. The portfolio will be cut in half by the time we start Social Security.

Unfortunately, because our society is conditioned to focus on total assets, both of these clients originally had a misplaced understanding of their financial health.

Client #1 always said they needed to work until they're 70, because they've always been under the impression that "you have to have a million dollars to retire." I meet with them twice a year to remind them that they're in great shape, but I'm still not sure they believe me yet.

Client #2 was incredibly confident in his plan to retire at 60, and it took several meetings to convince him that this was a bad idea. He couldn't fathom that his two million dollars wasn't going to be enough and he was certain that something was wrong with my math. But after seeing the numbers in black and white, it finally started to sink in. Realistically, their options are either for him to work longer than he'd planned, or make some significant changes to their lifestyle. Or maybe a combination of the two. They haven't exactly decided which of those unpleasant options they'll choose, but at least they now know what's realistic and what's not.

Here's the bottom line. Don't make assumptions about your financial health, one way or the other, until you have a clear understanding of what metrics are important.

Unless you have two donkeys. In that case, you are very rich.

# ABOUT THE AUTHOR

John Stillman is the founder of Carolina Wealth Stewards, a Registered Investment Advisor in Durham, NC, and the co-founder of Third Wheel Media, a media company that helps financial advisors and other professionals around the country with their marketing presence on radio, TV, and the web.

He graduated from the University of North Carolina at Chapel Hill in 2006 and currently lives in Durham, NC, with his wife Molly, daughter Lilly, son Amos, and dogs Tater and Audrey.

Made in the USA
Columbia, SC
19 August 2017